Choosing Sentences

A sentence must tell a whole idea. Read each group of words. Color the balloons:
purple – **a sentence**
green – **not a sentence**

 Yesterday we went to the State Fair.

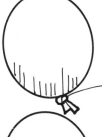 We saw lots of

 It was fun to ride on the ferris wheel.

I was excited when I won a big

My favorite food was cotton candy.

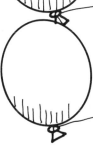 Next year we are

D1369589

IF5062 Basic Writing Skills

Choosing Sentences

Name _____

A sentence must tell a whole idea. The computer is programmed to write sentences. But even computers can make mistakes. Read each group of words.
Trace the computer strips:
red— **a sentence**   yellow— **not a sentence**

Eight bands marched in the parade.

The plane flew close to

The deer ran deep into the woods.

The fog covered most

The loud noise frightened the kids.

The town bell rings every day.

Choose **one** yellow strip. Add words to make a sentence.

_____.

Making Sentences

Name _____

A sentence tells a whole idea. Cut and paste each picture and group of words to make a sentence.

The chef has made

The kids saw

My new travel book

The envelope contained

a beautiful rainbow.

is full of great pictures.

a red and white valentine.

a huge wedding cake.

3

IF5062 Basic Writing Skills

Making Sentences

Name _____

A sentence tells a whole idea. Cut and paste the words to make five sentences about the picture.

Bob and Sam hope

They want to earn

Every Saturday they will

The boys will put

In three months, they

their money in the bank.

money by mowing yards.

to buy bicycles this summer.

each mow four yards.

will have enough money.

Telling Sentences

A telling sentence begins with a capital letter and ends with a period. Write each telling sentence correctly on the lines.

Camp Rules

1. everyone goes to breakfast at 6:30 each morning

   _____

2. only three people can ride in one canoe

   _____

3. each person must help clean the cabins

   _____

4. older campers should help younger campers

   _____

5. all lights are out by 9:00 each night

   _____

6. everyone should write home at least once a week

   _____

Telling Sentences

Name _____

A telling sentence begins with a capital letter and ends with a period. Look at each TV picture. Write a telling sentence about each program.

_____

_____

_____

_____

_____

_____

_____

_____

_____

_____

_____

_____

Asking Sentences

An asking sentence begins with a capital letter and ends with a question mark. Write each question correctly on the line.

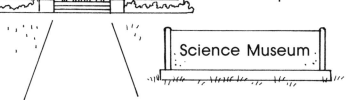

1. is our class going to the Science Museum

_____

2. will we get to spend the whole day there

_____

3. will a guide take us through the museum

_____

4. do you think we will see dinosaur bones

_____

5. is it true that the museum has a mummy

_____

6. can we take lots of pictures at the museum

_____

7. will you spend the whole day at the museum

_____

Asking Sentences

An asking sentence begins with a capital letter and ends with a question mark. Look at the picture. Write five asking sentences about the picture.

_____

_____

_____

_____

_____

Kinds of Sentences

A telling sentence ends with a period. [.]

An asking sentence ends with a question mark. [?]

Read each sentence. Put the correct mark in each [ ].

1. Would you like to help me make an aquarium [ ]

2. We can use my brother's big fish tank [ ]

3. Will you put this colored sand in the bottom [ ]

4. I have three shells to put on the sand [ ]

5. Can we use your little toy boat, too [ ]

6. Let's go buy some fish for our aquarium [ ]

7. Will twelve fish be enough [ ]

8. Look, they seem to like their new home [ ]

9. How often do we give them fish food [ ]

10. Let's tell our friends about our new aquarium [ ]

Kinds of Sentences

Name _____

A telling sentence makes a statement.
An asking sentence asks a question.
Read each sentence. Look at the pictures. Cut and paste each
sentence in the correct space: A—asking   T—telling

Telling   Asking

A

T

A

T

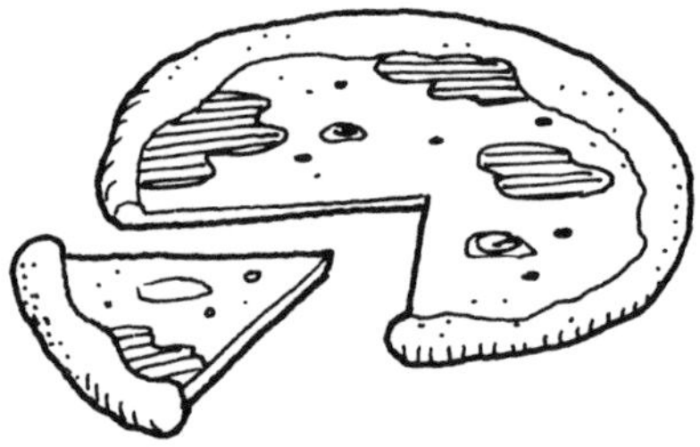

A

T

What is your favorite food?

The weather is sunny and warm.

How many legs does a spider have?

The spider has eight legs.

Pizza is my favorite food.

What is the weather today?

Choosing Sentences

A sentence must tell a whole idea. Read the letter from John to his granddad. Put a circle around each group of words which is not a sentence.

— John —

Dear Granddad,

    I have a wonderful surprise to tell you about. Mom and Dad gave me a pony for my birthday. She is brown with. I have named her Little One. Yesterday I rode her for. She likes to eat sugar cubes. It is fun to.

    You will like Little One when you come to visit us. I will show you how I. Please come to see us soon. We miss.

                 Love,
                 John

Look at the circled words. Add words and rewrite each group as sentence.

1. _____.

2. _____.

3. _____.

4. _____.

5. _____.

Writing Sentences

Name _____

A sentence must make sense. Read each sentence. Put an **X** on the **two** words which do not belong. Write the corrected sentence on the lines below.

Yard Sale   My neighbor is orange having a yard very sale.

1. _____

_____

She is snow selling lots of old things phone.

2. _____

_____

A man until is buying five candle old books.

3. _____

_____

My brother is buying an salt old checkers it game.

4. _____

_____

Two ladies pull are buying an old touch toy chest.

5. _____

_____

IF5062 Basic Writing Skills

Writing Sentences

Name _____

A sentence begins with a capital letter.
A telling sentence ends with a period.
An asking sentence ends with a question mark.

Come to the Fourth of July Picnic.
Town Park—All Day

Write three **telling** sentences about the picture.

_____

_____

_____

Write three **asking** sentences about the picture.

_____

_____

_____

Writing Sentences

Name _____

A sentence can tell or ask something. Choose two pictures. Color, cut and paste the pictures. Write two telling sentences and one asking sentence about each picture.

telling: _____

_____

asking: _____

_____

telling: _____

_____

telling: _____

_____

asking: _____

_____

telling: _____

_____

Writing Sentences

A sentence has a beginning and an ending.
Draw a line to match the beginning and
ending of each sentence.

Kerry's mother   who are sick or hurt.

She helps many animals   that she is a big help.

Every Saturday Kerry   food and soft blankets.

She gives the animals   be a vet someday, too.

Her mother says   is a veterinarian.

Kerry hopes to   helps her mother at work.

Completing Sentences

Name _____

A sentence needs a good beginning. Read the ending for each sentence. Write a beginning for each sentence. Draw a picture of the sentence.

1. _____ and wrapped it in blue paper with a yellow bow.

2. _____ and put them in a large vase filled with water.

3. _____ so he ran quickly to call the fire department.

Making Sentences

Sentences can be just for fun. Cut and paste a word in each space. Read each sentence. Draw a picture of each sentence.

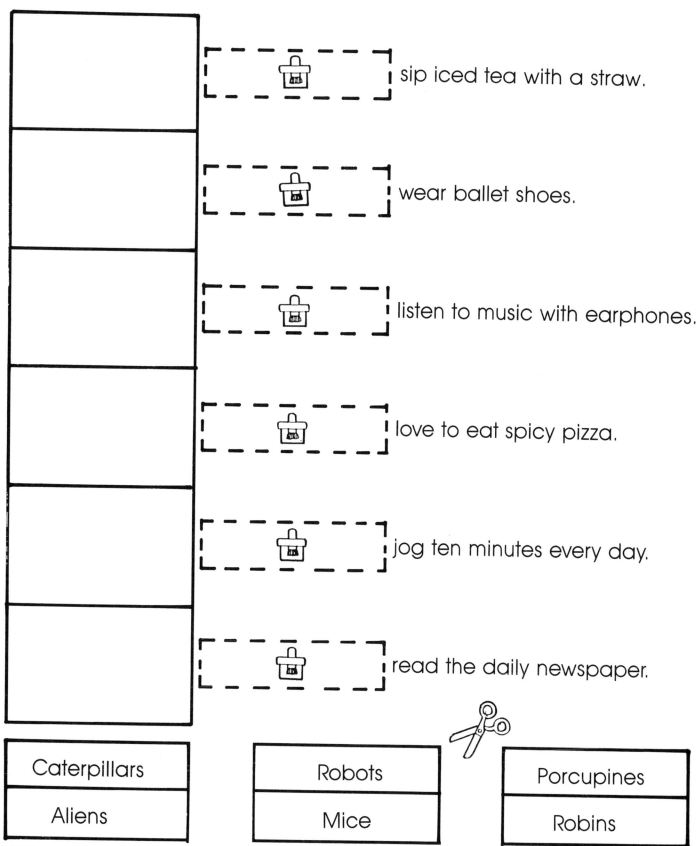

sip iced tea with a straw.

wear ballet shoes.

listen to music with earphones.

love to eat spicy pizza.

jog ten minutes every day.

read the daily newspaper.

| Caterpillars |
| Aliens |

| Robots |
| Mice |

| Porcupines |
| Robins |

Sentence Building

Name _____

A sentence can tell more and more. Read the sentence parts. Write a word on each line to make the sentence tell more. Draw a picture of the last sentence.

The Crunchy Carrot   **Supermarket**

1. Lynn went to the _____.

2. Lynn and _____ went to the _____

3. Lynn and _____ went to the _____

   to buy a jar of _____.

4. Lynn and _____ went to the _____

   to buy a jar of _____ and two packages of

   _____.

5. Lynn and _____ went to the _____

   to buy a jar of _____ and two packages of

   _____ for their _____.

Making Sentences

A sentence must make sense. Read the beginning of each sentence. Circle the correct ending. Write another ending for the sentence.

My family   and closed the door as he left.

is going to the game tonight.

My family _____

Our team   has lost only one game this year.

put her keys in her purse.

Our team _____

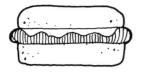

I like to   if the bus does not arrive on time.

eat hot dogs and chips at the game.

I like to _____

The cheerleaders   jump and yell for our team.

every day after school.

The cheerleaders _____

Basketball   is my family's favorite sport.

and placed it in the box.

Basketball _____

Completing Sentences

Sentences need special words that describe. Read each sentence. Write a describing word on each line. Draw a picture to match each sentence.

High Mountain

The _____ flag waved over the _____ building.

A _____ lion searched for food in the _____ jungle.

We saw _____ fish in the _____ aquarium.

Her _____ car was parked by the _____ van.

The _____ dog barked and chased the _____ truck.

The _____ building was filled with _____ packages.

Writing Sentences

A sentence needs special words. Cut and paste two words by the picture they tell about. Write a telling and an asking sentence about each picture. Use one of the words in each sentence.

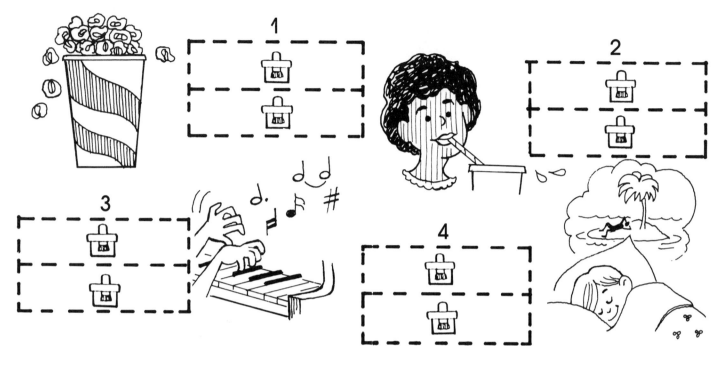

1. telling _____

   asking _____

2. telling _____

   asking _____

3. telling _____

   asking _____

4. telling _____

   asking _____

dream	thirsty	sleepy	music
yummy	tune	crunchy	refreshing

Proofreading

Name _____

A good sentence does not have any mistakes. Read each sentence carefully. Can you find the mistakes? Write the number of mistakes in the . Write the sentence correctly on the line.

 our school is having a carnival in October

_____

 my mom is helping me with my homework?

_____

 would you like to play. after school today.

_____

 I am having a birthday party next Thursday?

_____

can we ride the. subway in the city.

_____

 have you met the new boy in our class

_____

         IF5062 Basic Writing Skills

Writing Sentences

Name _____

Sentences can tell about special times. Every season of the year is special. Write four words to tell about each season. Use the words to write two sentences about each season.

Four Seasons

Winter

1. _____
2. _____
3. _____
4. _____

Spring

1. _____
2. _____
3. _____
4. _____

Summer

1. _____
2. _____
3. _____
4. _____

Fall

1. _____
2. _____
3. _____
4. _____

Winter _____
_____

Spring _____
_____

Summer _____
_____

Fall _____

Better Sentences

Special words can make a better sentence. Read each sentence. Write a word on each line to make the sentences more interesting. Draw a picture of your sentence.

The skater won a medal.

1. The _____ skater won a _____ medal.

The jewels were in the safe.

2. The _____ jewels were in the _____ safe.

The airplane flew through the storm.

3. The _____ airplane flew through the _____ storm.

A fireman rushed into the house.

4. A _____ fireman rushed into the _____ house.

The detective hid behind the tree.

5. The _____ detective hid behind the _____ tree.

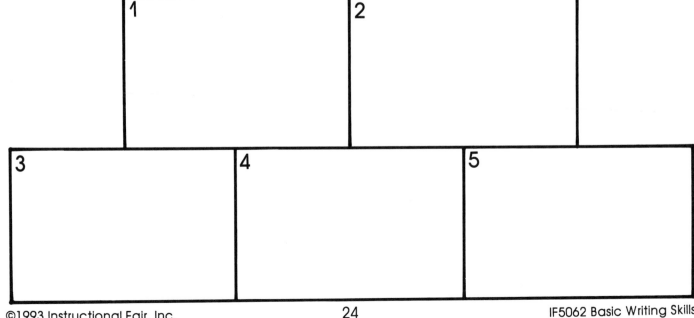

Writing Sentences

A sentence can tell about feelings. Cut and paste each face by the correct word. Write two sentences: a sentence to tell **how** the person feels, and a sentence to tell **why** he/she feels that way. Give each person a name.

 happy

1. _____

2. _____

 grouchy

1. _____

2. _____

 surprised

1. _____

2. _____

25   IF5062 Basic Writing Skills

Completing Sentences

ho?

hen?

Name _____

A sentence can tell exactly what is happening. Read each sentence. Write a word or words to tell **who** or **when** on each line.

1. Mary's little _____ is starting her first day at
   Who?

   school _____ .
   When?

2. Aunt _____ is moving to Florida _____ .
   Who?   When?

3. It was almost _____ when _____ arrived at
   When?   Who?

   the party.

4. Mr. _____ wants to meet with the
   Who?

   soccer team next _____ .
   When?

5. We have an appointment at _____ to have our teeth
   When?

   checked by Dr. _____ .
   Who?

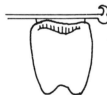

6. _____ and _____ are going to the movies
   Who?   Who?

   _____ instead of _____ .
   When?   When?

Sentence Building

Name _____

 Who? What? When? Where? **A sentence can tell more and more.** Write a word or words on each line to make the sentence tell more and more. Draw a picture of the last sentence.

1. The _____ bought a _____ .
          Who?   What?

   The _____ bought a _____ at the
          Who?   What?

   _____ .
      Where?

   The _____ bought a _____ at the
          Who?   What?

   _____ _____ .
      Where?   When?

2. My best _____ borrowed my _____ .
              Who?   What?

   My best _____ borrowed my _____ to
              Who?   What?

   take to the _____ .
                Where?

   My best _____ borrowed my _____ to
              Who?   What?

   take to the _____ _____ .
                Where?   When?

1	2

IF5062 Basic Writing Skills

Sentence Building

A sentence can tell more and more. Read the sentence parts. Write a word on each line to make the sentence tell more. Draw a picture of the last sentence.

1. The hikers saw a big _____.

2. The hikers saw a big _____ and a _____.

3. The hikers saw a big _____ and a _____

   behind the _____.

4. The hikers saw a big _____ and a _____

   behind the _____ as they returned from a

   _____.

5. The hikers saw a big _____ and a _____

   behind the _____ as they returned from a

   _____ late last _____.

Sentence Building

 **Tell me more.** **A sentence can tell more about something.** Read each sentence. Cut and paste words to make each sentence tell more.

1. Tom likes to go to the library.

   Tom likes to go to the library
   when

2. Sue's class went on a field trip.

   Sue's class went on a field trip
   where

3. Pete did not do his homework.

   Pete did not do his homework
   why

4. Will you meet me at the movies?

   Will you meet me at the movies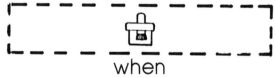
   when

5. Sarah is saving her money.

   Sarah is saving her money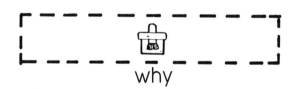
   why

| at five o'clock? | to the science fair. |
| to buy a new bike. | because he was sick. |

| every Saturday morning. |

Sentence Combining

Name _____

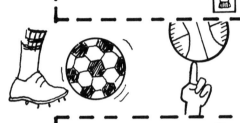

Two sentences can become one sentence. Read the two sentences. Cut and paste the sentence parts to make one sentence.

It snowed all day yesterday.
It snowed all day today.

⌐ ⌐ ⌐ ⌐ ⌐ ⌐ ⌐ and ⌐ ⌐ ⌐ ⌐

Muffin likes to play soccer.
Muffin likes to play basketball.

⌐ ⌐ ⌐ ⌐ ⌐ ⌐ ⌐ and ⌐ ⌐ ⌐ ⌐

I am flying to visit Grandmother.
I am flying to visit Grandfather.

⌐ ⌐ ⌐ ⌐ ⌐ ⌐ ⌐ and ⌐ ⌐ ⌐ ⌐

Our town has a big library.
Our town has a big museum.

⌐ ⌐ ⌐ ⌐ ⌐ ⌐ ⌐ and ⌐ ⌐ ⌐ ⌐

I am flying to visit Grandmother	museum.
basketball.	It snowed all day yesterday
Our town has a big library	Grandfather.
today.	Muffin likes to play soccer

Sentence Combining

Two sentences can become one sentence. Read the two sentences. Write them as one sentence.

The bird lives in a nest.
The bird lives in the tree.

The music teacher is wearing a blue dress.
The music teacher is wearing white pearls.

I will meet you at the park.
I will meet you by the balloon stand.

My first name is Brian.
My last name is Williams.

Patty is in the second grade.
Patty is in elementary school.

Sentence Combining

Name _____

Two sentences can become one sentence. Read the two sentences. Write them as one sentence by using the (word) between the two.

Example: I go to the library. I like to read books.
(because) I go to the library because I like to read books.

1. Our class sang songs. We waited for the bus to arrive.

 (while) _____
_____

2. I got dirty when I played soccer. I took a shower.

 (so) _____
_____

3. I may go to the movies. I may go skating.

 (or) _____
_____

4. I watched my TV program. I did my homework.

  (after) _____
_____

Sentence Completion

Sentences can tell why something happened. Read the beginning of each sentence. Complete each sentence by telling why something happened.

1. There is no school today **because** _____

_____.

2. I gave my friend a new record **because** _____

_____.

3. I have to go to the dentist today **because** _____

_____.

4. The old theater is being torn down **because** _____

_____.

5. The baseball game was called off **because** _____

_____.

6. We cannot see the moon tonight **because** _____

_____.

Making Sentences

A sentence can give special information. Read the directions for each note. Write one sentence that tells the correct information.

Write a note telling your mother where you are going after school.

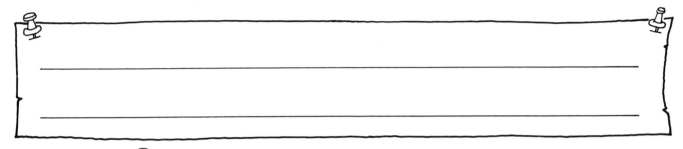

Write a note telling your teacher why you were not at school yesterday.

Write a note telling your mailman when you are going on vacation.

Write a note to your new neighbors offering to help them unpack.

Write a note asking your friend to go to the movies with you next Saturday.

Making Sentences

Sentences can tell about something special. Would you like to fly away for a fun trip? Write words about a trip on the plane. Use the words to write five sentences about the trip.

1. _____

2. _____

3. _____

4. _____

5. _____

Sentence Sequence

Sentences can tell how to do something. Read each step in taking a class nature walk. Write **1-5** in the O's to put the steps in order.

Nature Walk

○ Write a list of things you hope to see at this place.

○ After the walk, write about what you have seen.

○ Give everyone something from the list to look for.

○ Choose a place for the class to walk.

○ As you walk, talk about what you see.

Write five sentences that tell what **you** might see on a nature walk in the woods.

1. _____

2. _____

3. _____

4. _____

5. _____

Story Sequence

Sentences can tell about the order of events. Read each sentence. Write two sentences to tell what two things could happen next.

1. We arrived at Grandma's late that night.

2. _____

3. _____

1. Sally went to the shelter to choose a new pet.

2. _____

3. _____

1. The truck backed into the fruit stand.

2. _____

3. _____

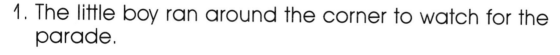

1. The little boy ran around the corner to watch for the parade.

2. _____

3. _____

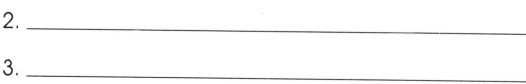

Story Sequence

Name _____

Sentences can tell a story. Read each sentence. Cut and paste the sentence that tells what happened next. Write a sentence that tells what **could** happen after that.

The sailors sailed through the foggy night.

The divers jumped from the boat into the water.

The fishermen threw their nets into the water.

| They swam down to the old sunken ship. |
| When the nets were heavy, they pulled them up. |
| Suddenly they saw a lighthouse far away. |

Sentence Sequence

Sentences can tell the order of events. Read each sentence. Look at the matching picture. Write the two missing sentences to complete the story.

First: The brave knight saw the dragon.

Next: _____

Last: _____

First: _____
Next: The boy rubbed the magic lamp.

Last: _____

First: _____

Next: _____
Last: The little girl waved good-bye to the unicorn.

Sentence Sequence

Sentences can tell a story. Color, cut and paste the pictures in **1-4** order to tell a story. Write a sentence on each line that tells what is happening in the pictures.

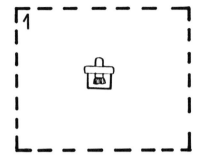

_____

_____

_____

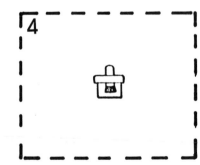

_____

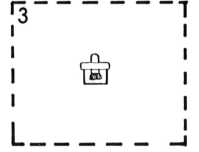

_____

_____

_____

_____

Speech Bubble

 A sentence can tell what someone is saying. Look at each picture. Write a sentence in the bubble that tells what the person is saying.

Writing Sentences

Sentences can tell much about you. Begin at the **START** sign and write sentences that tell all about you—how you look, your age, things you like to do, etc. Write as many sentences as you can going around and around the circle.

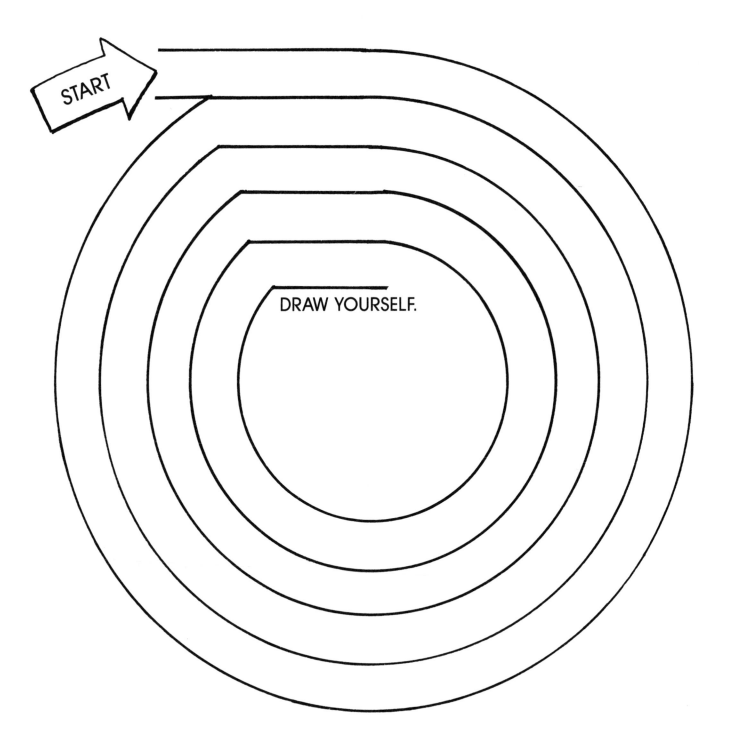

START

DRAW YOURSELF.

Brainstorming

Brainstorming can give you ideas for writing. Answer the questions below. Use the answers as ideas to help you write five sentences about your family.

My Family

How many people are in your family? _____

What are their names? _____

_____

Write two words that tell about each person.

_____ _____ _____ _____

_____ _____ _____ _____

What is your family's favorite meal? _____

What is your family's favorite TV show?

_____

My Family

1. _____

2. _____

3. _____

4. _____

5. _____

43 IF5062 Basic Writing Skills

Answer Key

Basic Writing Skills
Grade 2

Choosing Sentences   Name _____

A sentence must tell a whole idea. Read each group of words. Color the balloons:
purple – a sentence
green – not a sentence

- **purple** — Yesterday we went to the State Fair.
- **green** — We saw lots of
- **purple** — It was fun to ride on the ferris wheel.
- **green** — I was excited when I won a big
- **purple** — My favorite food was cotton candy.
- **green** — Next year we are

Page 1

Choosing Sentences   Name _____

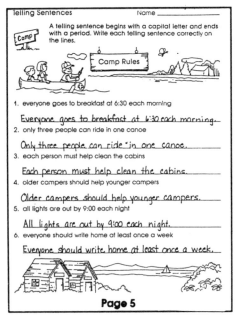

A sentence must tell a whole idea. The computer is programmed to write sentences. But even computers can make mistakes. Read each group of words. Trace the computer strips:
red– a sentence   yellow— not a sentence

- Eight bands marched in the parade. — **red**
- **yellow** — The plane flew close to
- The deer ran deep into the woods. — **red**
- **yellow** — The fog covered most
- The loud noise frightened the kids. — **red**
- **red** — The town bell rings every day.

Choose one yellow strip. Add words to make a sentence.

Answers will vary.

Page 2

Making Sentences   Name _____

A sentence tells a whole idea. Cut and paste each picture and group of words to make a sentence.

- The chef has made | a huge wedding cake.
- The kids saw | a beautiful rainbow.
- is full of great pictures.
- My new travel book | is full of great pictures.
- a red and white valentine.
- The envelope contained | a red and white valentine.
- a huge wedding cake.

Page 3

Making Sentences   Name _____

A sentence tells a whole idea. Cut and paste the words to make five sentences about the picture.

- Bob and Sam hope to buy bicycles this summer.
- They want to earn money by mowing yards.
- Every Saturday they will each mow four yards.
- The boys will put their money in the bank.
- In three months, they will have enough money.

their money in the bank. | money by mowing yards.
to buy bicycles this summer. | each mow four yards.
will have enough money.

Page 4

Telling Sentences   Name _____

A telling sentence begins with a capital letter and ends with a period. Write each telling sentence correctly on the lines.

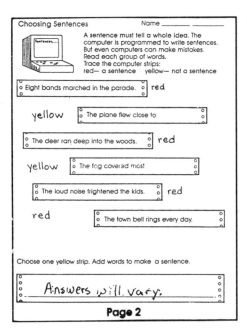

Camp Rules

1. everyone goes to breakfast at 6:30 each morning
Everyone goes to breakfast at 6:30 each morning.

2. only three people can ride in one canoe
Only three people can ride in one canoe.

3. each person must help clean the cabins
Each person must help clean the cabins.

4. older campers should help younger campers
Older campers should help younger campers.

5. all lights are out by 9:00 each night
All lights are out by 9:00 each night.

6. everyone should write home at least once a week
Everyone should write home at least once a week.

Page 5

Telling Sentences   Name _____

A telling sentence begins with a capital letter and ends with a period. Look at each TV picture. Write a telling sentence about each program.

Answers will vary.

Page 6

Asking Sentences   Name _____

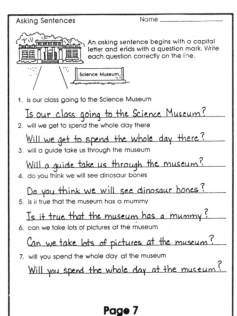

An asking sentence begins with a capital letter and ends with a question mark. Write each question correctly on the line.

Science Museum

1. is our class going to the Science Museum
Is our class going to the Science Museum?

2. will we get to spend the whole day there
Will we get to spend the whole day there?

3. will a guide take us through the museum
Will a guide take us through the museum?

4. do you think we will see dinosaur bones
Do you think we will see dinosaur bones?

5. is it true that the museum has a mummy
Is it true that the museum has a mummy?

6. can we take lots of pictures at the museum
Can we take lots of pictures at the museum?

7. will you spend the whole day at the museum
Will you spend the whole day at the museum?

Page 7

IF5062 Basic Writing Skills

Page 8

Asking Sentences Name _____

An asking sentence begins with a capital letter and ends with a question mark. Look at the picture. Write five asking sentences about the picture.

Answers will vary.
_____
_____
_____
_____

Page 8

Page 9

Kinds of Sentences Name _____

A telling sentence ends with a period. ⊡

An asking sentence ends with a question mark. ?

Read each sentence. Put the correct mark in each □

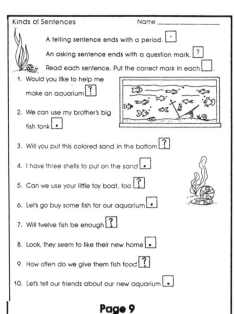

1. Would you like to help me make an aquarium ?

2. We can use my brother's big fish tank .

3. Will you put this colored sand in the bottom ?

4. I have three shells to put on the sand .

5. Can we use your little toy boat, too ?

6. Let's go buy some fish for our aquarium .

7. Will twelve fish be enough ?

8. Look, they seem to like their new home .

9. How often do we give them fish food ?

10. Let's tell our friends about our new aquarium .

Page 9

Page 10

Kinds of Sentences Name _____

A telling sentence makes a statement.   [Telling] [Asking]
An asking sentence asks a question.
Read each sentence. Look at the pictures. Cut and paste each sentence in the correct space: A—asking T—telling

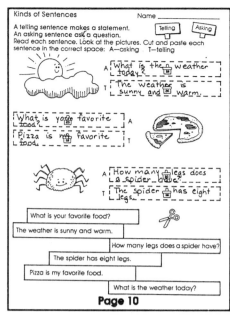

A What is the weather today?
T The weather is sunny and warm.

A What is your favorite food?
T Pizza is my favorite food.

A How many legs does a spider have?
T The spider has eight legs.

What is your favorite food?
The weather is sunny and warm.
How many legs does a spider have?
The spider has eight legs.
Pizza is my favorite food.
What is the weather today?

Page 10

Page 11

Choosing Sentences Name _____

A sentence must tell a whole idea. Read the letter from John to his granddad. Put a circle around each group of words which is not a sentence.

John

Dear Granddad,

I have a wonderful surprise to tell you about. Mom and Dad gave me a pony for my birthday. (She is brown with.) I have named her Little One. (Yesterday I rode her for.) She likes to eat sugar cubes. (It is fun to.)

You will like Little One when you come to visit us. (I will show you how.) Please come to see us soon. (We miss.)

Love,
John

Look at the circled words. Add words and rewrite each group as a sentence. **Possible answers.**

1. She is brown with white spots.
2. Yesterday I rode her for an hour.
3. It is fun to have a pony.
4. I will show you how I brush her.
5. We miss you.

Page 11

Page 12

Writing Sentences Name _____

A sentence must make sense. Read each sentence. Put an X on the two words which do not belong. Write the corrected sentence on the lines below.

Yard Sale My neighbor is oran̶g̶e̶ having a yard va̶r̶y̶ sale.

1. My neighbor is having a yard sale.

She is sn̶o̶w̶ selling lots of old things ph̶o̶n̶e̶.

2. She is selling lots of old things.

A man un̶t̶i̶l̶ is buying five can̶o̶e̶ old books.

3. A man is buying five old books.

My brother is buying an sh̶i̶r̶t̶ old checkers ga̶m̶e̶ game.

4. My brother is buying an old checkers game.

Two ladies pi̶l̶l̶ are buying an old to̶u̶c̶h̶ toy chest.

5. Two ladies are buying an old toy chest.

Page 12

Page 13

Writing Sentences Name _____

A sentence begins with a capital letter.
A telling sentence ends with a period.
An asking sentence ends with a question mark.

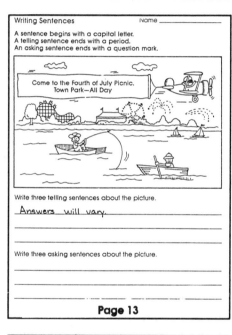

Come to the Fourth of July Picnic.
Town Park—All Day

Write three telling sentences about the picture.

Answers will vary.
_____
_____

Write three asking sentences about the picture.

_____
_____

Page 13

Page 14

Writing Sentences Name _____

A sentence can tell or ask something. Choose two pictures. Color, cut and paste the pictures. Write two telling sentences and one asking sentence about each picture.

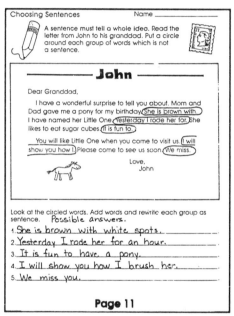

telling: Answers will vary.
asking: _____
telling: _____

telling: _____
asking: _____
telling: _____

Visit the Beautiful Sandy Beach Hotel
• Great Food
• Pool • Music • Fun

Sunny Supermarket

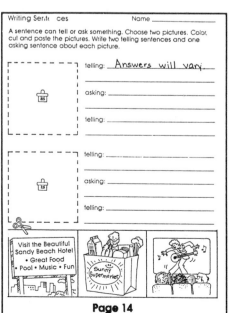

Page 14

Page 15

Writing Sentences Name _____

A sentence has a beginning and an ending. Draw a line to match the beginning and ending of each sentence.

Kerry's mother — is a veterinarian.
She helps many animals — who are sick or hurt.
Every Saturday Kerry — helps her mother at work.
She gives the animals — food and soft blankets.
Her mother says — that she is a big help.
Kerry hopes to — be a vet someday, too.

Page 15

Page 16

Completing Sentences Name _____

A sentence needs a good beginning. Read the ending for each sentence. Write a beginning for each sentence. Draw a picture of the sentence.

1. Answers will vary. _____ and wrapped it in blue paper with a yellow bow.

2. _____ and put them in a large vase filled with water.

3. _____ so he ran quickly to call the fire department.

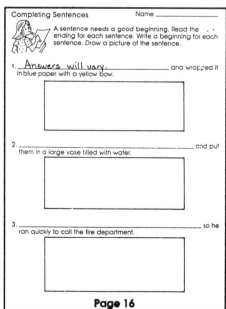

Page 16

©1993 Instructional Fair, Inc.   45   IF5062 Basic Writing Skills

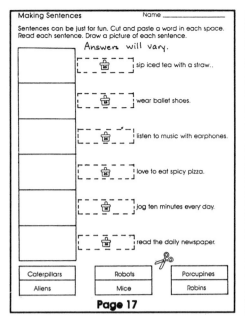
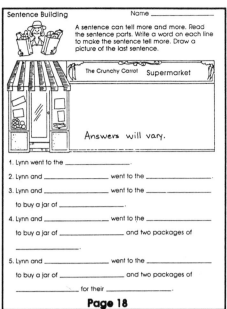
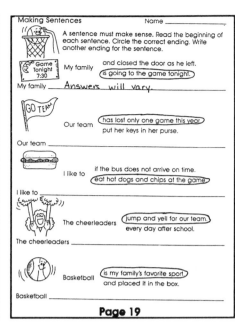

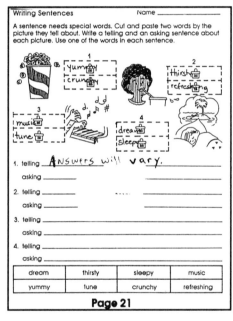
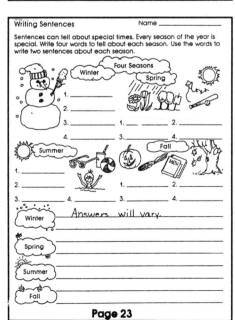

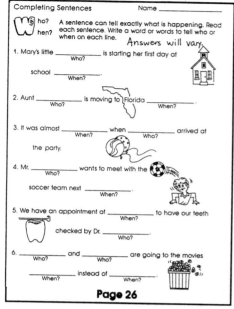

Completing Sentences   Name _____

Who? When? A sentence can tell exactly what is happening. Read each sentence. Write a word or words to tell who or when on each line.

Answers will vary.

1. Mary's little _____ (Who?) is starting her first day at

school _____ (When?)

2. Aunt _____ (Who?) is moving to Florida _____ (When?)

3. It was almost _____ (When?) when _____ (Who?) arrived at

the party.

4. Mr. _____ (Who?) wants to meet with the

soccer team next _____ (When?)

5. We have an appointment at _____ (When?) to have our teeth

checked by Dr. _____ (Who?)

6. _____ (Who?) and _____ (Who?) are going to the movies

_____ (When?) instead of _____ (When?)

Page 26

Sentence Building   Name _____

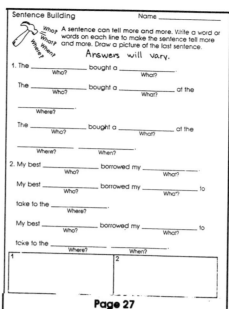

Who? What? When? Where? A sentence can tell more and more. Write a word or words on each line to make the sentence tell more and more. Draw a picture of the last sentence.

Answers will vary.

1. The _____ (Who?) bought a _____ (What?)

The _____ (Who?) bought a _____ (What?) at the

_____ (Where?)

The _____ (Who?) bought a _____ (What?) at the

_____ (Where?) _____ (When?)

2. My best _____ (Who?) borrowed my _____ (What?)

My best _____ (Who?) borrowed my _____ (What?) to

take to the _____ (Where?)

My best _____ (Who?) borrowed my _____ (What?) to

take to the _____ (Where?) _____ (When?)

1	2

Page 27

Sentence Building   Name _____

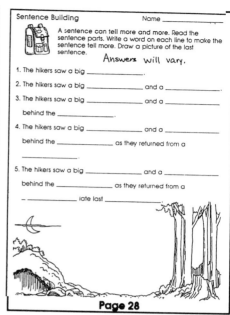

A sentence can tell more and more. Read the sentence parts. Write a word on each line to make the sentence tell more. Draw a picture of the last sentence.

Answers will vary.

1. The hikers saw a big _____

2. The hikers saw a big _____ and a _____

3. The hikers saw a big _____ and a _____

behind the _____.

4. The hikers saw a big _____ and a _____

behind the _____ as they returned from a

_____.

5. The hikers saw a big _____ and a _____

behind the _____ as they returned from a

_____ late last _____.

Page 28

Sentence Building   Name _____

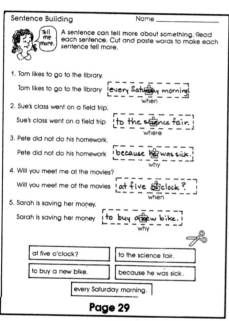

Tell me more. A sentence can tell more about something. Read each sentence. Cut and paste words to make each sentence tell more.

1. Tom likes to go to the library.

Tom likes to go to the library | every Saturday morning |
when

2. Sue's class went on a field trip.

Sue's class went on a field trip | to the science fair. |
where

3. Pete did not do his homework.

Pete did not do his homework | because he was sick |
why

4. Will you meet me at the movies?

Will you meet me at the movies | at five o'clock? |
when

5. Sarah is saving her money.

Sarah is saving her money | to buy a new bike. |
why

at five o'clock?	to the science fair.
to buy a new bike.	because he was sick.
every Saturday morning.	

Page 29

Sentence Combining   Name _____

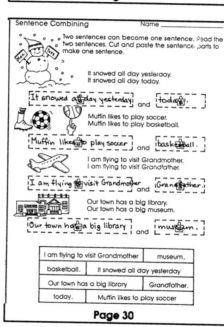

Two sentences can become one sentence. Read the two sentences. Cut and paste the sentence parts to make one sentence.

It snowed all day yesterday.
It snowed all day today.

| It snowed all day yesterday | and | today. |

Muffin likes to play soccer.
Muffin likes to play basketball.

| Muffin likes to play soccer | and | basketball. |

I am flying to visit Grandmother.
I am flying to visit Grandfather.

| I am flying to visit Grandmother | and | Grandfather. |

Our town has a big library.
Our town has a big museum.

| Our town has a big library | and | museum. |

I am flying to visit Grandmother	museum.
basketball.	It snowed all day yesterday
Our town has a big library	Grandfather.
today.	Muffin likes to play soccer

Page 30

Sentence Combining   Name _____

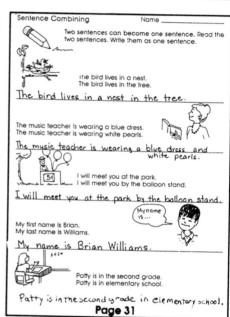

Two sentences can become one sentence. Read the two sentences. Write them as one sentence.

The bird lives in a nest.
The bird lives in the tree.

The bird lives in a nest in the tree.

The music teacher is wearing a blue dress.
The music teacher is wearing white pearls.

The music teacher is wearing a blue dress and white pearls.

I will meet you at the park.
I will meet you by the balloon stand.

I will meet you at the park by the balloon stand.

My first name is Brian.
My last name is Williams.

My name is Brian Williams.

Patty is in the second grade.
Patty is in elementary school.

Patty is in the second grade in elementary school.

Page 31

Sentence Combining   Name _____

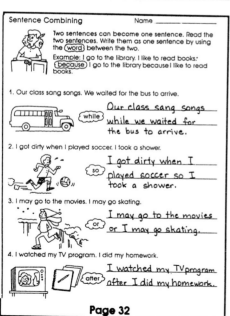

Two sentences can become one sentence. Read the two sentences. Write them as one sentence by using the word between the two.

Example: I go to the library. I like to read books.
(because) I go to the library because I like to read books.

1. Our class sang songs. We waited for the bus to arrive.

(while) Our class sang songs while we waited for the bus to arrive.

2. I got dirty when I played soccer. I took a shower.

(so) I got dirty when I played soccer so I took a shower.

3. I may go to the movies. I may go skating.

(or) I may go to the movies or I may go skating.

4. I watched my TV program. I did my homework.

(after) I watched my TV program after I did my homework.

Page 32

Sentence Completion   Name _____

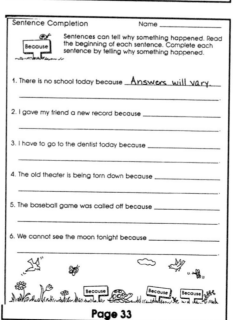

Because Sentences can tell why something happened. Read the beginning of each sentence. Complete each sentence by telling why something happened.

1. There is no school today because Answers will vary

2. I gave my friend a new record because _____

3. I have to go to the dentist today because _____

4. The old theater is being torn down because _____

5. The baseball game was called off because _____

6. We cannot see the moon tonight because _____

Page 33

Making Sentences   Name _____

A sentence can give special information. Read the directions for each note. Write one sentence that tells the correct information.

Write a note telling your mother where you are going after school.

Answers will vary

Write a note telling your teacher why you were not at school yesterday.

Write a note telling your mailman when you are going on vacation.

Write a note to your new neighbors offering to help them unpack.

Write a note asking your friend to go to the movies with you next Saturday.

Page 34

        IF5062 Basic Writing Skills

Making Sentences   Name _____

Sentences can tell about something special. Would you like to fly away for a fun trip? Write words about a trip on the plane. Use the words to write five sentences about the trip.

1. _Answers will vary._
2. _____
3. _____
4. _____
5. _____

Page 35

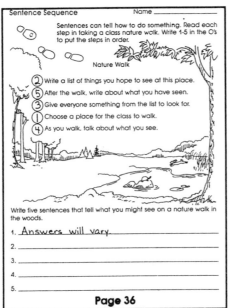

Sentence Sequence   Name _____

Sentences can tell how to do something. Read each step in taking a class nature walk. Write 1-5 in the O's to put the steps in order.

Nature Walk

② Write a list of things you hope to see at this place.
⑤ After the walk, write about what you have seen.
③ Give everyone something from the list to look for.
① Choose a place for the class to walk.
④ As you walk, talk about what you see.

Write five sentences that tell what you might see on a nature walk in the woods.

1. _Answers will vary._
2. _____
3. _____
4. _____
5. _____

Page 36

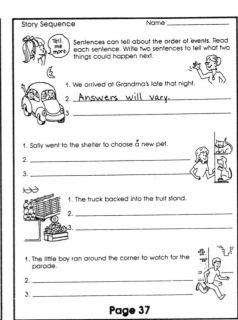

Story Sequence   Name _____

Sentences can tell about the order of events. Read each sentence. Write two sentences to tell what two things could happen next.

1. We arrived at Grandma's late that night.
2. _Answers will vary._

1. Sally went to the shelter to choose a new pet.
2. _____
3. _____

1. The truck backed into the fruit stand.
2. _____
3. _____

1. The little boy ran around the corner to watch for the parade.
2. _____
3. _____

Page 37

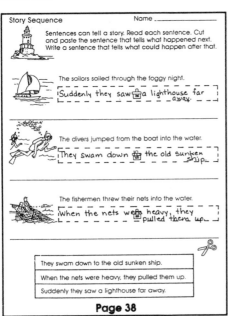

Story Sequence   Name _____

Sentences can tell a story. Read each sentence. Cut and paste the sentence that tells what happened next. Write a sentence that tells what could happen after that.

The sailors sailed through the foggy night.
Suddenly they saw a lighthouse far away.

The divers jumped from the boat into the water.
They swam down to the old sunken ship.

The fishermen threw their nets into the water.
When the nets were heavy, they pulled them up.

They swam down to the old sunken ship.
When the nets were heavy, they pulled them up.
Suddenly they saw a lighthouse far away.

Page 38

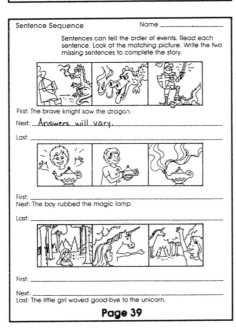

Sentence Sequence   Name _____

Sentences can tell the order of events. Read each sentence. Look at the matching picture. Write the two missing sentences to complete the story.

First: The brave knight saw the dragon.
Next: _Answers will vary._
Last: _____

First: _____
Next: The boy rubbed the magic lamp.
Last: _____

First: _____
Next: _____
Last: The little girl waved good-bye to the unicorn.

Page 39

Sentence Sequence   Name _____

Sentences can tell a story. Color, cut and paste the pictures in 1-4 order to tell a story. Write a sentence on each line that tells what is happening in the pictures.

Sentences will vary.

Page 40

Speech Bubble   Name _____

A sentence can tell what someone is saying. Look at each picture. Write a sentence in the bubble that tells what the person is saying.

Sentences will vary.

Page 41

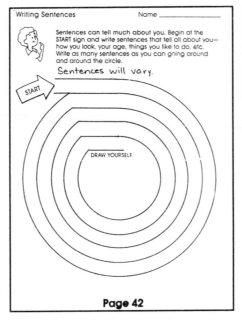

Writing Sentences   Name _____

Sentences can tell much about you. Begin at the START sign and write sentences that tell all about you—how you look, your age, things you like to do, etc. Write as many sentences as you can going around and around the circle.

Sentences will vary.

START

DRAW YOURSELF.

Page 42

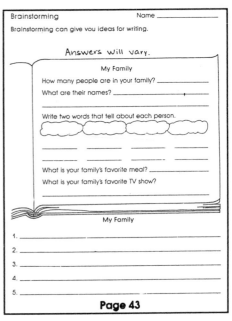

Brainstorming   Name _____

Brainstorming can give you ideas for writing.

Answers will vary.

My Family

How many people are in your family? _____
What are their names? _____

Write two words that tell about each person.

_____
_____

What is your family's favorite meal? _____
What is your family's favorite TV show? _____

My Family

1. _____
2. _____
3. _____
4. _____
5. _____

Page 43